Digital Marketing Mastery

Crafting Effective Strategies for Online Success

James Macaulay

Table of contents

Introduction

In an era defined by rapid developments in technology and the ever-expanding reach of the Internet, mastering the art of digital marketing has become a must for individuals and enterprises. As the digital landscape continues to evolve, it has evolved to include a wide range of platforms, tools, and techniques, making it a dynamic and multifaceted field that requires a deep understanding and strategic approach. "Masters in Digital Marketing:
Building Effective Strategies for Online Success" is a comprehensive journey into the heart of this transforming field, providing readers with an in-depth exploration of the principles, tactics, and strategies that define success in the digital arena.

This book is your roadmap to tackling the complexities of digital marketing, equipping you with the knowledge and skills to excel in the increasingly competitive online landscape. Whether you're an aspiring digital marketer looking to launch a successful career, a seasoned professional looking to hone your skills, or a business owner looking to launch your brand to the next level, this book will give you the insights and strategies you need. demand. prosperous. In the "Mastering Digital Marketing" pages, you will learn about the latest trends and best practices in digital marketing, from search engine optimization (SEO) and marketing content to social media advertising and email marketing. You'll dive into the psychology of online consumer behavior and learn how to create engaging, data-driven campaigns that resonate with your target audience. Additionally, you will gain a deep understanding of the tools and technologies that support your digital marketing efforts, allowing you to leverage data analytics, automation, and emerging technologies to your advantage.

Beyond the technical aspects, this book emphasizes the importance of developing authentic and resonant brand stories. It explores the art of storytelling in digital marketing, illustrating how compelling stories can foster meaningful connections with customers, build brand loyalty, and drive sustainable growth. Along the way, you'll encounter real-world case studies, practical tips, and actionable insights from industry experts, providing you with real-world lessons you can take advantage of. You can apply it immediately to your digital marketing efforts.

As you embark on your "Digital Marketing Mastery" journey, you will not only gain the knowledge but also the confidence to skillfully navigate the ever-changing digital landscape. Whether you're looking to strengthen your brand, grow your organization's online presence, or simply stay ahead of digital trends, this book is your essential guide to mastering the art of digital marketing and effective strategizing for online success.

"Masters in Digital Marketing:
Building Effective Strategies for Online Success" brings together insights and expertise from industry leaders and digital marketing pioneers. As the subtitle suggests, the book This book is not just about theory and concepts but also about translating them into concrete strategies that deliver tangible results.

In today's hyper-connected world, where the digital landscape is often the primary battleground for businesses seeking consumer attention, mastering the intricacies of digital marketing is essential. This book acknowledges the dynamic nature of the online domain, recognizing that what worked yesterday may not work tomorrow. Therefore, it not only provides a solid foundation but also equips you with the tools to adapt to the ever-changing digital ecosystem.

One of the key themes explored in this book is the concept of holistic digital marketing. It emphasizes the importance of synergy across various digital channels and platforms, demonstrating how a coordinated and integrated approach can maximize the impact of your marketing efforts. From search engine marketing (SEM) to social media management, from email campaigns to influencer partnerships, this book will guide you in crafting a comprehensive digital strategy that aligns with your objectives.

Furthermore, "Digital Marketing Mastery" goes beyond the technical aspects and delves into the realm of creativity and innovation. It encourages readers to think outside the box, inspiring the development of innovative campaigns that capture the imagination of their target audience. You'll learn how to leverage emerging trends like augmented reality, chatbots, and voice search to stay ahead of the digital marketing game.

Throughout the book, you will also find a series of practical exercises and checklists that allow you to immediately apply the knowledge gained. Whether you are a student looking to enter the world of digital marketing, an entrepreneur looking to build a formidable online presence, or a marketing professional looking to lead your team to success, This hands-on activity will help you solidify your understanding and hone your strategy. SKILL.

In short, "Mastering Digital Marketing:
Building Effective Strategies for Online Success" is the
definitive guide to helping you conquer the ever-changing
digital frontier. It provides a comprehensive, up-to-date
resource for understanding, strategizing, and exporting
excellence in the world of digital marketing. By the time you
finish reading this book, you'll be well equipped to not only
navigate the digital landscape but also lead your digital
marketing efforts with confidence and skill, ultimately
achieving success. online in an increasingly competitive
digital sector.

Chapter One
Understand the digital landscape

Navigating the digital wilderness:

An overview
In a world increasingly defined by the pervasive influence of technology, our lives are increasingly intertwined with the digital landscape. From the moment we wake up to the sound of our smartphone alarms to our late-night social media scrolls, our existence is intertwined with the digital world. It is not just an aspect of modern life; it is the fabric on which our society is woven.

Digital revolution:
The term "digital landscape" conjures up images of an ever-expanding virtual terrain, a vast and complex wilderness beyond our understanding. This is not just a technological change but a revolution that has changed the way we communicate, work, shop, learn, and even perceive reality. To understand this landscape is to embark on a journey through the most transformative period in human history.

Digital Desert:
Imagine the digital landscape, if you will, as a vast wilderness, filled with both opportunities and challenges. Like wilderness, it can be both beautiful and unforgiving, breathtaking in its diversity but terrifying in its complexity. It's where information flows like rivers and mountains of data tower above us. In this wilderness, we find ourselves

navigating a maze of interconnected trails, each leading to a new destination. Diverse terrain

The digital landscape is diverse and consists of different terrains, each with its characteristics. Its focus is on the social media sector, where billions of individuals share their thoughts, experiences, and cat videos. Here, trends are born, movements explode and influence is cultivated.

Venture further and you'll discover the e-commerce savanna, where online marketplaces and retailers vie for supremacy. It's where you can buy everything from the latest gadgets to exotic spices, all from the comfort of your own home. Then there's the search engine jungle, a vast land where algorithms wield immense power. This is where people search for answers, discover new information, or simply satisfy their curiosity. The rules of this jungle are constantly changing as search engines continually adapt to provide better results.

Virtual border:

In this digital wilderness, we also find the virtual frontier, where emerging technologies such as augmented reality, virtual reality, and the Internet of Things (IoT) are reshaping our perception of reality. It's a place where imagination has no limits and where the lines between the real world and the virtual world blur. The importance of understanding

Understanding the digital landscape is not an option; it is a necessity. This not only affects individuals but also businesses, governments, and society as a whole. It shapes our economies, influences our politics, and determines the success or failure of businesses.

The way forward:
As we set out to explore this digital landscape, we will delve deeper into its different terrains, learn how to solve its challenges, and take advantage of its opportunities. We'll explore the technology behind it, the trends that drive it, and the strategies that lead to success. But this journey is about more than just practical knowledge; it's about capturing the profound impact of the digital revolution on our lives, culture, and future. It is about realizing that we are not mere spectators but active participants in the shaping of this landscape.

In the chapters that follow, we'll equip ourselves with the tools and information we need to thrive in the digital wild. We'll demystify the mysteries of search engine optimization, decode the secrets of viral content, and explore the ethical dilemmas posed by data privacy. Together, we will become digital explorers, charting a course through the uncharted territories of the digital frontier.

So buckle up, dear readers, because the journey ahead promises to be exciting, enlightening, and above all necessary in an age where understanding the digital landscape means understanding the world itself. Welcome to start your digital journey. Digital ecosystem
To truly understand the digital landscape, it is essential to grasp the concept of a large, interconnected ecosystem. In this ecosystem, websites are institutions and hyperlinks are circuits that circulate information. Search engines act as the ecosystem's neural network, helping us locate and retrieve data from its vast archives.

Think of social media platforms as bustling cities in this digital ecosystem. Each platform is a unique metropolis with its own culture, people, and dialect. Facebook, Twitter, Instagram, LinkedIn, and TikTok – each of these platforms represents a distinct corner of this digital universe, offering opportunities to connect, express yourself and make an impact.

Beyond social cities are digital markets, similar to the bustling trading posts of yore. Here, companies compete for the attention and loyalty of consumers. E-commerce giants

like Amazon and Alibaba have become the digital equivalent
of the global marketplace, while countless small online stores
flood the digital streets, offering appropriate products and
services.

The data abyss:
In this digital landscape, data is the lifeblood. Every click,
search, and interaction creates a digital footprint. Our personal
preferences, habits, and behaviors are all meticulously
recorded. The digital landscape, like an informed observer,
notes our choices, learns our preferences, and anticipates our
needs. It's a paradoxical relationship: we offer data in
exchange for convenience and personalization, but we also
grapple with concerns about privacy and security.

This ever-widening data gap forms the foundation of modern
marketing and informs the algorithms that decide the content
we encounter. It is the fuel of artificial intelligence, powering
chatbots, recommendation engines, and predictive analytics.

Sailing in the desert:
Understanding the digital landscape requires developing a
new set of skills. It's like learning to navigate a dense forest:
you need to be able to read the terrain, identify landmarks,
and choose the best path to follow.

We'll explore the art of digital storytelling, which is at the
heart of successful online communication. Creating stories
that resonate with audiences in this context can be the
difference between obscurity and virality. Search engine
optimization (SEO) will become a household term as we

delve deeper into the tactics and strategies to ensure your digital presence doesn't get lost in the vastness of the Internet. The complexities of pay-per-click advertising, content marketing, and email campaigns will be demystified.

Ethical dilemmas:
Yet as we navigate the digital wilderness, we also face the ethical dilemmas it brings. The collection and use of personal data, the spread of misinformation, and the potential for technology

addiction raise profound questions about our responsibilities as digital citizens.

Conclusion:
In this introductory chapter, we have only scratched the surface of the digital landscape. It is an ever-evolving world, offering both extraordinary opportunities and daunting challenges. But as we embark on this exploration together, remember that understanding the digital landscape is more than just acquiring knowledge; it's about gaining the knowledge and wisdom to navigate this brave new world with confidence and determination.

So, as we venture deeper into this wild digital world, let curiosity be your guide and critical thinking your trusted guide. With each chapter that unfolds, we will equip ourselves with the skills, knowledge, and ethics needed to navigate this vast and ever-changing landscape. Welcome to your digital adventure, where understanding is the first step to mastery.

Chapter Two
Identify your target audience

In business and marketing, one of the fundamental keys to success is understanding your target audience. Whether you're launching a new product, running a marketing campaign, or developing content, identifying your target audience is an essential step that shapes your entire strategy. This comprehensive summary will delve deeper into the importance of audience identification, the methods and factors involved, and the challenges to consider.

Why identify your target audience
Connections for Successful Marketing:
The main reason to define your target audience is the direct correlation between audience understanding and marketing success. By identifying the individuals or groups most likely to be interested in your product or service, you can tailor your marketing efforts to effectively resonate with them. This leads to higher conversion rates, increased customer retention, and ultimately better ROI (return on investment).

Avoid a one-size-fits-all approach:
Trying to please everyone often leads to diluting your message and marketing resources. By identifying your target audience, you can avoid a one-size-fits-all approach and focus your efforts on a specific group that shares similar characteristics and interests. This not only saves time and resources but also improves the relevance of your message.

Successful case studies:

Many businesses and organizations have achieved significant success after effectively identifying and targeting their audiences. For example, consider the rise of health-tracking apps. Initially, they targeted health-conscious people who wanted to track their workouts and diet. By understanding the preferences and behaviors of this niche audience, these apps have grown exponentially, serving more fitness enthusiasts.

Demographic data:
Demographics refers to quantifiable data about your audience, including age, gender, location, income level, education level, and more. Understanding demographics is important because they form the basis for creating audience personas and tailoring your marketing efforts.

How to collect demographic data:
Collecting demographic data can be done through a variety of means, such as surveys, social media insights, website analytics, and customer databases. Collecting accurate data is essential to creating an accurate representation of your audience.

Create a character:
After collecting demographic data, you can create audience personas and fictional representations of your typical customers. These personas help you humanize your audience and make more informed decisions about content, messaging, and product development.

Psychology:

Psychology helps gain a deeper understanding of your audience's attitudes, values, and lifestyles. This layer of information is just as important as demographics because it provides insight into what drives your audience's decision-making process.

Conduct surveys and research:
Psychographic data can be obtained through surveys, focus groups, and market research. By asking questions about beliefs, interests, and lifestyle choices, you can build a more comprehensive picture of your audience. Create detailed audience profiles
Detailed audience profiles combine demographic

and psychographic data to create a comprehensive representation of your target segment. These profiles include not only age, gender, and location but also motivations, aspirations, and weaknesses.

Behavior and preferences:
Understanding your audience's behavior and preferences is key to creating content and offers that resonate.

Analyze consumer behavior:
By analyzing your audience's online behavior, such as what they search for, click on, or buy, you'll gain valuable insights into their interests and needs. Tools like Google Analytics and social media monitoring can help adjust content and offers when you understand your audience's behavior and preferences, you can tailor your content, products, and services to meet their specific needs and desires. This personalization significantly increases the chances of conversion.
Challenges in object identification While identifying your target audience is important, it is not without its challenges. Some common pitfalls to be aware of include making assumptions without proper research, failing to adapt to changing audience dynamics, and falling victim to demographic stereotypes.

The evolving nature of audiences:
In the digital age, audiences are constantly evolving. What worked yesterday may not work tomorrow. Staying aware of your audience's preferences and habits is a continuous process.

Case-control study:
It is essential to learn from the mistakes of businesses that are struggling due to wrong assumptions about their audience. For example, a company targeting Millennials with products designed for the Baby Boomer generation will likely face many challenges.

Practical exercise Identify objects step by step
Segment:
Start by dividing your larger target audience into smaller segments based on demographics. For example, if you're marketing a fitness product, segment it by age, gender, and location. This segmentation helps you identify key subsets of your audience.

Psychological profile:
Go deep into the psychology of each segment. Conduct surveys or interviews to understand their values, preferences, and lifestyle choices. For example, are they fitness enthusiasts looking for quick results or individuals looking for long-term health?

Behavioral analysis:
Use tools like Google Analytics to analyze online behavior. Track what pages they visit on your site, what products they view, and how they interact with your content. Understandably, this data progresses in its direction

Create character:

Develop detailed audience portraits for each segment. These characters must have a lot of detail, including not only their age and gender but also their daily habits, challenges, and aspirations. Give each character a name and face to make them feel real.

 Prioritize:
Determine which audience segments are most promising and profitable. This involves evaluating factors such as segment size, purchasing power, and alignment with your brand values.

 Check and confirm:
Identifying your audience is an assumption. Continuously test and validate it with A/B testing and market research. If you notice a segment isn't responding as expected, be prepared to modify your approach.

Spreadsheets and templates:
Providing spreadsheets and templates to guide your audience research can be extremely helpful to readers. These resources may include:

Demographic data collection table:
A structured form to collect demographic data from a variety of sources. Psychological survey questionnaire:
A set of questions designed to extract psychological information from your audience.

Character model:
Blank forms where readers can fill in details about their audience.

Audience segmentation matrix:
A matrix helps readers visualize different audience segments and their attributes.

Validation Checklist:
The checklist helps evaluate the accuracy and effectiveness of the identified target audience.

The process of identifying objects is ongoing
Targeting is not a one-time task but an ongoing process. As your business grows and market dynamics change, your target audience may change too. It's important to continually monitor and update your audience profile to stay relevant.
The role of flexibility and adaptation

Flexibility is key in audience targeting. Sometimes unexpected opportunities arise or external factors affect your audience. Be prepared to adjust your strategies and personality accordingly. Conclusion
Identifying your target audience is a fundamental step in any successful marketing and sales strategy. It allows you to personalize your messaging, optimize your resources, and increase the efficiency of your efforts. Additionally, this is an iterative process that needs to be revisited as your business grows and your audience grows. In the chapters that follow, we'll explore how to craft messaging that resonates with your identified audience, creating powerful connections that get results.

Chapter Three
Content creation and optimization

Introduction

In today's digital age, content reigns supreme. From the blog posts we read and videos we watch to the images we see and podcasts we listen to, content surrounds us in an ever-expanding online world. It is the lifeblood of the Internet, a medium of communication and a bridge that connects individuals, businesses, and organizations with their audiences.

This chapter delves into the art and science of "content creation and optimization." We embark on a journey through the multifaceted landscape of creating, refining, and delivering content that not only engages but thrives in the vast digital ecosystem. As the saying goes, "content is king," but its reign is not without challenges and complications. The importance of this chapter lies in exploring the symbiotic relationship between content creation and optimization. Content creation is the creative spark that sparks ideas and creates stories that resonate with readers, viewers, or listeners. Optimization, on the other hand, is the strategic driver that ensures that this content reaches its target audience effectively, making it visible amid the digital noise.

Whether you're an aspiring content creator, a seasoned marketer, or a business owner looking to improve your online presence, this chapter will give you the knowledge and tools you need. needed to navigate a dynamic world of content.

We'll uncover the secrets to understanding what your audience wants, planning a content strategy that aligns with your goals, creating engaging, shareable content, optimizing it for search engines, distributing that content across platforms, and ultimately measuring its impact. Upcoming chapters will provide actionable insights, practical tips, and real-life examples to guide you on your content journey. Whether you're writing blog posts, producing videos, designing infographics, or engaging with your audience on social media, the principles you learn here are universally applicable.

In a world where information is abundant and attention spans are short, mastering content creation and optimization is not a luxury but a necessity. Let's embark on this enlightening journey together and explore the potential of content that goes viral, resonates deeply and ultimately stands the test of digital time.

Understand your audience

One of the fundamental pillars of successful content creation and optimization is a deep understanding of your audience. Your audience isn't just a bunch of anonymous internet users; they are real people with unique interests, needs, and behaviors. To create content that truly connects, resonates, and drives results, you need to invest time and effort to understand them.Here's why understanding your audience is essential:

Custom content:

Knowing your audience allows you to create content that directly addresses their interests, problems, and aspirations. This personalized approach fosters stronger connection and engagement.

Relevance:
Relevant content is more likely to attract and keep your audience's attention. When you know what's important to them, you can deliver content that meets their expectations.

Audience:
Creating detailed audience personas helps you visualize typical members of your audience. This involves demographics, interests, behaviors, and challenges. These personas serve as guiding personas for your content strategy.

Problem-solving:
Understanding your audience's problems and questions allows you to position your content as a solution. You become a trusted resource in your niche or industry. Content Orientation:
Audience insights drive your content strategy. They help you choose the right topic, format, and distribution channel.

Commitment and loyalty:
When your content consistently meets your audience's needs, you'll drive engagement and build brand loyalty. Satisfied audiences are more likely to come back for more.
In this chapter, we'll explore techniques and tools to dig deeper into audience psychology, from conducting audience research to building audience personas. This knowledge will be the compass that guides your content creation and optimization journey, ensuring that every piece of content you create is relevant to the people who matter most:
your audience.

Content planning and strategy

Creating effective content doesn't happen by accident; it is the result of carefully considered planning and content strategy. This important stage lays the foundation for success in the world of digital content. Here's why content planning and strategy is important:

Clear objectives:

A strategic content plan starts with clearly defined goals. Are you looking to increase website traffic, generate leads, increase brand awareness, or engage more deeply with your audience? Setting clear goals is the first step in your content journey. Consistency:
A content calendar keeps you on track and ensures a continuous flow of content. Consistency is key to building and maintaining trust with your audience.

Target content:
Understanding your audience (as discussed earlier) allows you to tailor your content to their interests. Your strategy should determine the type of content that will resonate the most with your audience.

SEO integration:
Content planning should incorporate search engine optimization (SEO) considerations. This involves keyword research and optimization, helping your content rank higher in search engine results.

Asset distribution:
The tactical approach allows assets to be allocated efficiently. Whether it's time, budget, or people, knowing where to invest is essential to maximize ROI.

Adaptability:
Your content strategy should be flexible, allowing you to adapt to changing trends, audience behavior, and industry changes.

In upcoming chapters, we'll dive deeper into the specifics of content planning and strategy, exploring how to set SMART goals, create a content calendar, choose the right content format, and integrate Integrate SEO seamlessly. These skills will enable you to create content that not only meets your goals but also resonates with your audience, paving the way for success in the digital landscape.

Content creation

At the heart of any successful content strategy is the art and craft of content creation. This is where your ideas take shape, your message comes to life, and your storytelling skills shine. Content creation is a tangible expression of your brand's personality and expertise, and it plays a central role in engaging your audience. Here's why it's so important:

Quality issues:
High-quality content is the foundation of any successful online presence. It's not just about words or images; it is about providing value, information, or entertainment that leaves a lasting impression.

Public participation:
Compelling content will capture your audience's attention, motivate them to read, watch, or listen, and encourage them to take action, whether it's sharing, subscribing, or making a purchase.

Consistency:
Creating consistent content will build trust and credibility with your audience. When they know they can count on your regular, valuable content, they'll be more likely to come back for more.

Stories:
Suggested stories are a powerful tool in content creation. They allow you to connect with your audience on an emotional level, making your brand more accessible and memorable.

Flexibility:
Content creation spans a variety of formats, from blog posts to videos, infographics, podcasts, and more. Understanding which format resonates best with your audience is part of the creative process.

In the next chapters, we'll go into detail about content creation. We'll explore techniques for creating catchy titles, compelling introductions, and maintaining a consistent tone. Whether you're a writer, designer, videographer, or content creator of any kind, this information will help you hone your skills and create outstanding content in the digital landscape.

Search engine optimization (SEO)

In the digital age where information is at our fingertips, search engine optimization (SEO) is the compass that directs content to audiences. SEO involves optimizing your online content and websites to improve their visibility on search engines like Google, Bing, and Yahoo. Here's why SEO is an essential aspect of content creation and optimization:

Visibility and discoverability:
Technical SEO helps your content and website rank higher in search engine results pages (SERPs). As your content becomes more visible, users will actively search for related information that is more likely to be discovered.

Free transportation:
Organic, organic traffic is driven to your website through SEO. This means you don't just rely on ads to attract visitors; instead, your content appears naturally in search results.

User experience:
SEO isn't just about pleasing search engines; it's also about improving the user experience. Well-optimized content is user-friendly, loads quickly, and is mobile-friendly.

Keyword strategy:
Effective SEO involves researching and strategically using keywords that are relevant to your content. This helps your content align with user intent and stand out in the competitive online space.

Authority and reputation:
High-level content is often considered more authoritative and trustworthy by users. SEO can help build your brand's reputation as a trusted source of information.

Continuous evolution:
SEO is not a single task. it's a dynamic field that changes depending on search engine algorithms and user behavior. Staying up to date with SEO best practices is critical to long-term success.

Over the next few chapters, we'll dive deeper into the world of SEO, exploring on-page and off-page optimization techniques, keyword research, and best practices for making your content search engine friendly. Understanding and applying SEO principles is essential to ensure your valuable content reaches the right audience across the vast digital landscape.

Content distribution and promotion

Creating great content is just the first step in your journey to connecting with your audience. Content distribution and promotion are equally essential parts of your content strategy. Here's why they're important:

Reach and visibility:
Content syndication ensures that your content reaches a wider audience. This involves sharing your content across different channels, including social media platforms, email, and content syndication. This increased reach increases the visibility of your content.

Public participation:
Promoting your content will positively engage your audience. Simply creating quality content is not enough; you should also encourage sharing, comments, and discussions to foster a sense of community around your brand.

Amplify the impact:
Syndication and promotion amplify the impact of your content. They help you maximize the ROI of your content by ensuring it doesn't go unnoticed.

Cross-platform presence:
In the digital age, audiences are fragmented across many different platforms. Effective distribution and promotion means being present where your audience spends their time

online, whether that's on social networks, forums, or industry-specific sites.

Consistency:
Sharing and promoting content regularly will help your audience interact and become aware of the products your brand offers. This builds trust and encourages more visits.

Paid promotions:
In addition to organic distribution, paid promotion through ads can further expand the reach of your content and target specific demographics.

In the chapters that follow, we'll explore strategies and tactics for effective content distribution and promotion. From leveraging social media to email marketing, guest posting, and paid advertising, you'll learn how to get your content in front of people's eyes and make a splash in the digital realm. These skills are essential for turning your content into a powerful tool for engaging your audience and growing your brand.

Analysis and Optimization

In the world of content creation and optimization, knowledge is power, and that knowledge comes from analysis. Analytics and optimization are the two pillars that help your digital strategy continuously improve. Here's why they're necessary:

Decisions based on data:

Analytics provide valuable insight into how your content is performing. You can track metrics like website traffic, user engagement, conversion rates, and more. This data allows you to make informed decisions about what's working and what needs improvement.

Continuous improvement:
Optimization is a continuous process by analyzing data, you can identify areas where your content and strategy can be improved. Whether it's fine-tuning your content approach or fine-tuning your distribution channels, optimization will ensure you're always aiming for better results.

Measuring ROI:
Analytics allows you to measure the return on investment (ROI) of your content efforts. You can determine which pieces of content generate the most value and adjust your strategy accordingly.

Audience information:
Analytics can reveal valuable insights into audience behavior
and preferences. This knowledge helps you tailor your content
to better meet your audience's needs.

Adapt to trends:
The digital landscape is constantly evolving. Analytics helps
you stay ahead of trends and changes in user behavior,
allowing you to adjust your strategy accordingly.

Target alignment:
By setting clear goals and tracking progress through analytics,
you ensure your content strategy stays aligned with your
overall goals. In the following chapters, we'll explore how to
effectively use analytics tools to collect data, interpret key
metrics, and apply optimization techniques. These skills are
vital to ensuring your content continues to evolve, deliver
value, and stay relevant in the dynamic digital landscape.

Content maintenance and updates

Creating engaging content is just the beginning of your
content journey. To truly thrive in the digital landscape, you
must also prioritize maintaining and updating content. Here's
why this ongoing process is important:

Relevance over time:
In a fast-paced world, content can quickly become outdated.
Regular maintenance ensures your content stays relevant,
accurate, and up to date.

Benefits of SEO:
Search engines favor fresh content. By updating and expanding existing content, you can improve its ranking and visibility in search engines.

Improve user experience:
Visitors appreciate accurate and up-to-date information. Keeping your content fresh will improve user experience and build trust with your audience. Take advantage of new trends: Content maintenance allows you to incorporate emerging trends, technologies, or developments in your field, demonstrating your industry expertise.

Reuse opportunities:
Updated content can be reused in different formats or used as the basis for new content, maximizing your content investment.

Fixes:
Regular maintenance helps you identify and fix errors, broken links, or problems in your content, ensuring a smooth user experience.

In the following chapters, we'll explore strategies for effectively maintaining and updating content. You'll learn how to identify outdated content, prioritize updates, and maintain an archive of content that continues to provide value to your audience over time. Performing content maintenance ensures that your digital presence remains dynamic, competent, and evergreen.

Conclusion

In the ever-changing digital landscape, content creation, and optimization are two pillars of success for individuals, businesses, and organizations. As we reach the pinnacle of this exploration, it is essential to reflect on the deeper meaning of these interconnected practices and the transformative impact they can have out for your digital journey.

The journey "Content creation and optimization" is a journey to the heart of digital communication, where ideas are transformed into words, images, and videos that engage, educate, and inspire excitement. In this conclusion, let us distill the main points that summarize the essence of this chapter:

Content is your voice:
Content is your voice in the digital realm. It's how you connect with your audience, convey your message, and stand out among the online information noise.

Audience-Centric Approach:
Understanding your audience is the compass that guides your content journey. By recognizing their needs, preferences, and pain points, you create content that resonates deeply.

Strategy Matters:
Content planning and strategy provide direction and purpose to your efforts. Well-defined objectives, a content calendar, and SEO integration are the cornerstones of a successful strategy.

Creativity and Quality:
Content creation is both an art and a science. Create engaging stories, maintain high quality, and use storytelling techniques to engage your audience.

SEO drives visibility:
Search engine optimization (SEO) ensures that your content isn't hidden in the vast digital landscape. Keywords, on-page and off-page optimization, and user-friendly content play a central role in your content's visibility.

Distribution and promotion:
Content distribution and promotion will expand the reach of your content. Engage with your audience through social

media, email marketing, and other channels to foster a sense of community.

Data-Driven Decisions:
Analytics and optimization are your compass and map. They provide insights, measure ROI, and guide continuous improvement in your content strategy.

Evolving with Time:
Content maintenance and updates are essential for remaining relevant and competitive. Keep your content fresh, accurate, and aligned with the latest trends.

In the dynamic world of digital content, one constant remains:
the need for adaptation and evolution. Content creation and optimization are not static processes but dynamic ones, requiring continuous learning, testing, and adaptation. As you embark on your content journey, remember that success is determined not only by the destination but also by the growth, learning, and connections made along the journey.

In short, "Content creation and optimization" is a journey without a final destination. It's a constant exploration of creativity, strategy, data, and connecting with audiences. By applying the knowledge learned in this chapter, you will confidently navigate the digital realm, making your content a powerful force for engagement, impact, and growth in a Digital is always changing.

Chapter Four
Social media marketing strategy

The marketing landscape has been completely changed by the advent of social media platforms. In this chapter, we dive deeper into the complexities of social media marketing strategies, exploring the ever-evolving tactics businesses use to attract, convert, and retain audiences. their goals in the digital age.

Understanding social media platforms:

Social media platforms are not one size fits all. Each platform has distinctive content formats, user bases, and engagement dynamics. Successful social media marketing begins with a thorough understanding of these nuances. Businesses should research and identify the platforms that best suit their brand and audience.

Set clear goals:

Before embarking on a social media marketing campaign, it's important to establish clear and measurable goals. Whether it's increasing brand awareness, driving website traffic, or increasing sales, setting specific goals will guide your strategy and help you measure success.

Content creation:

Content is the lifeblood of social media marketing. High-quality, engaging content is essential to attract and maintain your audience's attention. This includes a combination of text, images, videos, and user-generated content. Tailor your content to your target demographic and align it with your brand message.

Build and maintain community:

Social media can be used both ways, not just as a broadcast channel. Successful brands actively engage with their audiences, responding to comments, questions, and feedback. Moving your organization in a new direction will foster trust and loyalty. Paid advertising:

Social media platforms offer powerful advertising options, allowing businesses to target specific demographics with precision. Paid advertising can complement organic efforts by reaching a broader audience and generating immediate results.

Influencer Marketing:

Collaborating with influencers who have the right audience can enhance your brand's reach and credibility. However, it's important to choose influencers whose values align with your brand and whose audience matches your target demographic.

Analyze and make decisions based on data:

Social media platforms create awareness through unlimited information and valuable discovery tools. Regularly tracking key metrics like engagement rate, click-through rate, and conversion rate allows marketers to refine their strategies and optimize their campaigns for better results.

Staying Up-to-Date:

Social media has to do with dynamism as it could always happen to be in constant change. New features, algorithms, and trends emerge regularly. Marketers must stay up-to-date with the latest developments and be agile in adapting their strategies to remain relevant.

Crisis Management:

The speed and reach of social media can amplify both positive and negative events. Businesses need to have a crisis management plan in place to address any PR issues promptly and professionally.

Ethical considerations:

As social media marketing evolves, ethical considerations become increasingly important. Brands must be transparent, honest, and responsible in their online presence to maintain audience trust.

Timing and content consistency:

Consistency is key to social media marketing. Developing a content calendar helps maintain a regular publishing schedule, ensuring that your audience can expect and look forward to your content. This calendar should align with your marketing goals and incorporate current and relevant topics.

User-generated content:

Encouraging your audience to create and share content related to your brand can be a powerful strategy. User-generated content not only serves as social proof but also deepens the connection between your brand and customers.

A/B testing:

Testing is fundamental in social media marketing. A/B testing allows you to compare different variations of content, headlines, ad copy, or even posting times to determine what resonates most with your audience and create better results.

Localization and personalization:

Tailoring your social media content to specific regions or demographics can significantly improve engagement. Personalization doesn't stop at just using the recipient's name; this involves providing content that directly meets the interests and needs of individuals.

Report:

One of the powerful tools for engaging an audience
emotionally is storytelling. Creating compelling stories
around your brand, products, or values can leave a lasting
impression and make your brand more relatable. Mobile
Optimization:

With the majority of social media users accessing platforms
via mobile devices, it is important to optimize your content
for mobile use. Make sure your images, videos, and website
are mobile-friendly for a seamless experience.

Competitive analysis:

Researching your competitors' social media strategies can
provide valuable insights. Analyze content, engagement
tactics, and audience demographics to identify opportunities
for differentiation and improvement.

Community Management:

Dedicated community managers play a vital role in social
media marketing. They monitor conversations, respond
quickly to customer questions or concerns, and foster a
positive online environment around your brand.

Building long-term relationships:

While social media can be a platform for short-term
campaigns, it's equally important to focus on building

long-term relationships. Cultivating a loyal customer base can lead to repeat business and advocacy.

Compliance with laws and regulations:

Navigating the legal and regulatory landscape of social media marketing is crucial. Make sure your campaigns comply with advertising standards, data protection laws, and platform-specific guidelines to avoid legal complications.

Conclusion:

In an era dominated by social media, mastering effective marketing strategies on these platforms is essential for businesses that want to thrive in the digital age. The chapter on "Social Media Marketing Strategy" emphasizes the importance of a well-thought-out approach, creative content, community engagement, and data-driven decision-making for success in the dynamic world of social media marketing. By continuously adapting to the changing landscape and adhering to ethical principles, businesses can harness the power of social media to connect with audiences, drive growth, and achieve success long-term work.

Chapter Five
The basics of email marketing

Email marketing remains the cornerstone of your digital marketing strategy, providing a direct and personalized way to interact with your audience. In this chapter, we explore the essential principles and strategies behind effective email marketing campaigns. From building your subscriber list to creating engaging content and optimizing delivery, mastering these essential elements is critical to success.

Build a quality subscriber list:

Permission-based marketing:
Successful email marketing starts with permission. Building a subscriber list of people who voluntarily sign up is essential to maintain trust and avoid spam complaints. Registration form and incentives:
Using well-placed signup forms on your website or landing page, along with offers like discounts or exclusive content, can encourage visitors to sign up.

Dual registration:
Implementing a double opt-in process ensures subscribers confirm their interest, reducing the risk of fake or inactive emails.

Segmentation and personalization:

Targeted messages:

Segmenting your email list based on demographics, behavior, or interests allows you to send personalized messages tailored to specific audience segments.

Custom content:
Personalization is more than just addressing the subscriber by name. This involves personalizing email content based on personal preferences and purchase history. Create engaging content:

Subject line:
A compelling subject line is the first impression of your email. It should be short, engaging, and relevant to the content of the email.

Valuable content:
Your email content should provide value, whether through informative articles, exclusive offers, or entertaining stories.

Call to action (CTA):
Every email should contain a clear, compelling CTA to guide subscribers to take the desired action, whether it's making a purchase, registering for an event, or sharing content.

Design and Responsiveness:

Responsive design:
Emails must be optimized for different devices to ensure they look and work well on desktop and mobile.

Visual appeal:
Use visually appealing layouts, images, and fonts that align
with your brand style guide.

A/B testing:

Test variations:
A/B testing allows you to test different elements in your
emails, such as subject lines, CTAs, images, and content, to
determine which elements resonate best with your audience.

Delivery Ability:

Spam compliance:
Make sure your emails comply with anti-spam regulations by
including an unsubscribe link, and physical address, and
avoiding misleading subject lines.

Sender's reputation:
Maintain a positive sender reputation by consistently sending
relevant, non-spam content and promptly handling subscriber
complaints or bounces.

Analysis and Data:

Performance tracking:
Use an email marketing platform to track open rates,
click-through rates, conversion rates, and unsubscribe rates.
To tackle your email strategies, analyze the data first.

Automation and drip campaigns:

Emails are triggered over time:
Automation allows you to send emails based on subscriber
behavior or triggers, such as welcome emails, abandoned cart
reminders, or post-purchase follow-ups.

Drip campaign:
A drip campaign is an automated email series that nurtures
leads or attracts new customers over time.

Compliance and legal considerations:

Data privacy:
Comply with data privacy laws, such as GDPR or
CAN-SPAM, by obtaining consent, providing opt-outs, and
protecting subscriber data.

Permissions and disclaimers:
Make it easy for subscribers to unsubscribe and fulfill their
requests quickly.

Continuous optimization:

Regularly review and optimize your email marketing strategies based on performance metrics, subscriber feedback, and industry trends.

Frequency and time:

This is crucial when the right balance of email frequency is perfect. Too many emails can lead to subscriber fatigue and high unsubscribe rates, while too few emails can cause your audience to forget about your brand.
Experiment with different send times and dates to determine when your subscribers respond fastest. Tools and analytics can help you determine optimal transit times.

Cleaning and maintenance list:

Invalid or inactive addresses should be removed regularly to clean up your mailing list. This practice improves deliverability and prevents your emails from being marked as spam.
Implement re-engagement campaigns to win back disengaged subscribers instead of immediately removing them from your list.

Multi-channel integration:

Email marketing should be integrated into your broader marketing strategy. Coordinate your email campaigns with other marketing channels like social media, content marketing, and advertising to create a cohesive customer experience. Abandoned cart recovery:

For e-commerce businesses, implementing automated abandoned cart recovery emails can help recover sales that may have been lost. It reminds customers who have added products to their cart but have not completed the transaction.

Customer lifecycle emails:

Develop a series of emails tailored to different stages of the customer lifecycle. This can include welcome emails, onboarding sequences, upsell or cross-sell emails, and loyalty rewards.

Crisis communication:

In times of crisis or unexpected events, email can be an essential communication tool. Inform subscribers about how your business is handling the situation, any changes in operations, and safety measures.

Compliance audit:

Conduct periodic compliance checks to ensure your email marketing complies with applicable regulations. Stay up to date with any changes in data protection law that may affect your strategy.

Conclusion:

Email marketing remains a powerful tool for businesses to connect with their audiences, drive engagement, and achieve their marketing goals. The "Email Marketing Essentials" chapter emphasizes the importance of building a quality subscriber list, personalizing content, designing visually appealing emails, and ensuring deliverability and compliance.Comply with legal regulations. By mastering these essential elements and continuously improving their email marketing efforts, businesses can leverage this versatile channel to foster customer relationships, increase conversions, and achieve Long-term marketing success.

Chapter Six
Search engine optimization (SEO) tactics

 SEO is an essential chapter in the field of digital marketing and online visibility. SEO refers to the process of optimizing a website or online content to improve its ranking on search engine results pages (SERPs). This chapter looks at different tactics and strategies that businesses and website owners can use to improve their online presence and attract organic search engine traffic money. Here are the full notes on this important chapter:

1. The importance of SEO:

SEO is important because it helps websites appear high in search results, thereby increasing their visibility to potential visitors. Higher rankings lead to increased organic (non-paid) traffic, which can result in more leads, customers, and revenue.

2. On-page SEO:

On-page SEO tactics focus on optimizing each website.
Key factors include optimizing titles, titles, meta descriptions, and content for relevant keywords.
Proper keyword research is essential to identify the phrases that potential visitors use in search queries.

3. SEO techniques:

Technical SEO involves optimizing website infrastructure for search engines.
This includes improving site speed, mobile-friendliness, XML sitemaps, and crawling fixes.
Structured data markup (schema markup) can make content easier for search engines to understand.

4. Off-page SEO:

Off-page SEO includes strategies to build a website's authority and credibility.
Backlink building is an important aspect, which aims to acquire relevant and high-quality links from other websites.
Social media marketing and online reputation management also play a role in off-page SEO.

5. Content marketing:

High-quality, relevant, and engaging content is crucial for SEO success. Content must meet user intent, answer questions, and provide value.
Regularly updated blogs, articles, videos, and infographics can improve SEO.

6. Local SEO:

Local SEO tactics target local businesses and aim to improve visibility in local searches.
This involves optimizing your Google My Business profile, gathering local citations, and collecting positive reviews.

7. User Experience (UX):

SEO is closely linked to user experience because search engines favor websites that provide a seamless and user-friendly experience.
Factors like mobile responsiveness, site structure, and page load times influence UX and SEO.

8. Monitoring and analysis:

SEO is an ongoing process and tracking progress is essential. Tools like Google Analytics and Google Search Console provide valuable insights into website performance and search traffic.

9. Update algorithm:

Search engines regularly update their algorithms, which affects SEO strategies.
Staying informed about these updates and adjusting tactics accordingly is important.

10. Ethical considerations:

- Ethical SEO practices are essential for long-term success.
– Avoid black hat SEO tactics like keyword stuffing, hiding,
and link buying as they can lead to penalties.

11. Keyword research:

Keyword research is the foundation of SEO. This involves
identifying specific words and phrases that potential users
enter into search engines.
Tools like Google Key Planner, SEMrush, and Ahrefs can
help you with keyword research.
The intent of the keyword (informational, navigational,
transactional) should be considered when choosing which
keywords to optimize.

12. Link building:

Focus on getting high-quality backlinks from reputable
sources within your organization. Backlinks (links from
different websites to your website) are a very important factor.
Guest posting, creating shareable content, and leveraging
online PR can help build backlinks.

13. Content optimization:

Content optimization involves making sure your content is not
only keyword-rich but also valuable and engaging.

(H1, H2, H3) should be used as title tags to design your
content. To improve user experience, multimedia elements
such as images and videos should be included.

14. Optimize voice search:

Voice search optimization is crucial due to the rise of
voice-enabled devices like Siri and Alexa. Voice search
queries tend to be more conversational, so it's important to
optimize for long-tail keywords and natural language.

15. Mobile Optimization:

Mobile compatibility is an important ranking factor as more
and more users access websites via mobile devices.
Implement responsive design and make sure your website
runs smoothly on smartphones and tablets.

16. Analyze user intent:

Understanding user intent is key to delivering relevant
content.
Different users have different purposes, such as searching for
information, making purchases, or finding local businesses.
Tailor your content to fit these intent categories.

17. Competitive analysis:

Analyzing your competitors' websites and SEO strategies can
provide insight into what works in your industry. Identify

gaps and opportunities to outperform your competitors in
search results.

18. Local SEO tactics:

For traditional businesses, local search optimization is
crucial.
This includes setting up and optimizing Google My Business,
creating local content, and managing online reviews.

19. E-A-T (Expertise, Authority, Trustworthiness):

Expertise, authority, and trustworthiness are valuable assets
exemplified by Google.
This is especially important for websites in fields like
healthcare and finance.
Highlight facts, certifications, and authoritative sources in
your content.

20. SEO tools and software:

There are many SEO tools and software available to help with analysis and optimization. These tools make it easy to track keywords, audit your website, analyze your competitors, and more.
In the ever-changing SEO landscape, it's essential to stay up to date with the latest trends and best practices. SEO is not a one-time effort; This requires continuous monitoring, adjustment, and adaptation to changes in algorithms and changes in user behavior. A well-executed SEO strategy can have a profound impact on a website's visibility, traffic, and overall online success.

In short, mastering SEO tactics is fundamental for businesses and website owners who want to succeed online. Effective SEO involves a comprehensive approach, including on-page, technical, off-page, content, and local strategies. Staying on top of industry trends and search engine algorithms is essential to maintaining and improving search rankings, ultimately leading to increased visibility, traffic, and success in search engines business.

Chapter Seven
Pay-per-click (PPC) advertising

 PPC advertising is an important chapter in the world of digital marketing, providing businesses with a powerful method to reach their target audience and achieve immediate results. This chapter explores PPC advertising in detail, including key principles, benefits, strategies, and best practices. Here are the full notes on this important chapter:

1. Introduction to PPC Advertising:

PPC advertising is a digital marketing model in which every time a user uses or clicks on an advertiser-owned ad, they are paid by the advertiser.
It is commonly used on search engines like Google and Bing, as well as social media platforms like Facebook and Twitter.

2. Main components of PPC:

The followings below are the main components of PPC.
Key word:
PPC campaigns are built around specific keywords or phrases that are relevant to a business or product.

Ad copy:
Creating compelling ad copy is crucial to attracting clicks.

Bidding:
Advertisers bid on keywords to determine ad placement.

High altitude:
Search engines use quality scores to evaluate ad relevance and user experience.

3. Benefits of PPC Advertising:

Immediate results:
PPC campaigns can generate traffic and conversions quickly.

Target:
Precise targeted by specific demographics, locations, and devices.

Measurable:
PPC provides detailed performance metrics for easy tracking and optimization.

Budget control:
Advertisers have full control over their daily and overall budgets.

4. Types of PPC advertising:

Search advertising:
Text ads are displayed on search engine results pages (e.g. Google Ads).

Show ads:
Visual advertising (banners, images) is displayed on sites in the network.

Advertising on social networks:
PPC advertising on social platforms like Facebook, Instagram,
and LinkedIn.

Shopping ads:
Product-specific ads are commonly used by e-commerce
businesses.

5. PPC campaign structure:

Well-structured campaigns are essential for PPC success.
Organize ads into ad groups based on related keywords and
topics.
Use negative keywords to exclude irrelevant traffic.

6. Keyword research:

A successful PPC campaign is essentially achieved through
continuous keyword research. The right keywords can be
identified using tools like Google Key Planner and SEMrush.
Consider long-tail keywords for more specific targeting.

7. Writing ads:

Create concise and engaging ad copy that meets user needs.
Incorporate keywords and highlight unique selling points.
Use ad extensions to provide more information.

8. Incentive management:

Bid competitively to ensure ad visibility.
Performance and competition rely on monitoring and
adjusting incentives.
Implement bidding strategies like manual, automatic, or target
CPA bidding.

9. Ad quality score and ranking:

Quality Score evaluates your ad's relevance, landing page
quality, and expected click-through rate.
Ad rank determines the position of the ad as well as the cost
per click.
High-quality ads with the right landing pages often achieve
better placement at a lower cost.

10. A/B testing and optimization:

 - Continuously test ad variations to improve performance.
- Experiment with titles, descriptions, landing pages and ad images.
- Optimize based on click-through rate (CTR) and conversion rate.

 11. Remarketing:

 - Retarget users who have interacted with your website or ads. - Create personalized ads to re-engage potential customers.

12. Analysis and Reporting:

 - Use analytics tools to track PPC performance.
- Track key metrics like CTR, conversion rate, ROI and cost per conversion.
- Make data-driven decisions to refine campaigns.
13. Budget management:

 - Set realistic budgets and allocate them effectively between campaigns.
- Performance is ensured by regularly reviewing and adjusting budgets.

 In short, PPC advertising is a dynamic and results-oriented approach to digital marketing. When done strategically, it can provide businesses with immediate visibility, targeted traffic, and measurable ROI. However, successful PPC campaigns

require monitoring, optimization, and a deep understanding
of audience behavior, making it a valuable skill for digital
marketers and Businesses want to thrive in the online market.

Chapter Eight
Analyze and make decisions based on data

Is an essential chapter of modern business and digital marketing. It emphasizes the importance of collecting, analyzing, and using data to make informed decisions. This chapter explores concepts, tools, and strategies related to data-driven decision-making. Here is a comprehensive note on this important topic:

1. Introduction to Data-Based Decision Making:

Data-driven decision-making is a process that relies on the collection and analysis of data to guide choices, strategies, and actions. It is widely applied in various industries to improve efficiency, productivity, and profitability.

2. Role of analysis:

Analytics is the process of systematically analyzing data to detect patterns, trends, and perceptions.
It provides businesses with a competitive advantage by helping them understand customer behavior, market dynamics, and operational efficiency.

3. Data collection and sources:

Data can be collected from a variety of sources including websites, mobile applications, social media, sensors, surveys, and more.

Data quality and accuracy are essential for meaningful analysis.

4. Main analysis tools and technologies:

Google Analytics:
A popular web analytics tool for tracking website traffic and user behavior.
Data visualization tools:
Tools like Tableau and Power BI help transform data into visual insights.
Machine Learning and AI:
Advanced algorithms can discover complex patterns and predictions.

5. Data type:

Structured data:
Organized and easily searchable data (e.g., database).

Unstructured data:
Data in raw form, such as text, images, and social media posts.

Big data:
Extremely large and complex data sets require specialized analysis tools and techniques.

6. Data preprocessing:

Removal of errors, inconsistencies, and outliers is performed once the data has completed cleaning and preprocessing. Normalization, transformation, and data regularization are common preprocessing steps.

7. Key indicators and KPIs:

Metrics and key performance indicators (KPIs) are essential to measuring success. Examples include conversion rate, customer acquisition cost (CAC), customer lifetime value (CLV), and churn rate.

8. A/B testing:

A/B testing (split testing) is a controlled experiment that compares two versions of a website, email, or marketing campaign.
This helps determine which version performs best based on specific metrics.

9. Predictive analytics:

Use predictive analytics to predict future outcomes using historical data and statistical algorithms
It is useful for demand forecasting, risk assessment, and predicting customer behavior.

10. Customer segmentation:

 - Customer segmentation based on demographics, behavior, or interests allows for more personalized and targeted marketing.

11. Privacy and data security:

 - Data protection and compliance with privacy regulations (e.g. GDPR, CCPA) are essential. - Implement security measures and obtain user consent for data collection.

12. Data-based decision-making process:

 - Identify goals and objectives.
- Collect relevant data.
- Data is analyzed using appropriate tools and technique
- Explain ideas and models. - Make wise decisions and actions.
- Monitor results and repeat if necessary.

13. Challenges in data-driven decision making:

- Data overload and complexity.
- Ensure accuracy and quality of data. - Privacy and ethical issues.
- Limited skills and resources.

14. Advantages of data-based decision-making:

 - Improve decision accuracy and efficiency.
- Improve operational efficiency and save costs. - Better understanding and connection with customers.
- Competitive advantage and innovation.

15. Case studies and examples:

 - Real-world examples demonstrate the impact of data-driven decisions in industries such as e-commerce, healthcare, finance, and marketing.

 In short, the era of data-driven decision-making is transformative for businesses and organizations. Data-driven strategies and analytics enable businesses to better understand their operations, customers, and markets, thereby making more effective decisions, increasing competitiveness, and improving overall performance. can. Mastering the art of collecting, analyzing, and leveraging data is essential for businesses that want to thrive in the digital age.

Chapter Nine
Building a Strong Online Brand

Is a pivotal chapter in the realm of digital marketing and business strategy. It explores the intricacies of establishing and nurturing a powerful brand presence in the digital landscape. This chapter encompasses essential principles, strategies, and best practices for creating and maintaining a compelling online brand. Here's a comprehensive note on this significant topic:

1. Introduction to Online Branding:

Online branding involves crafting a unique, recognizable, and memorable identity for a business, product, or service in the digital world. It includes the image, message, and overall perception created by the online audience.

2. The importance of online branding:

Online branding is very important for businesses:

 Make a difference from your competitors.
Build trust and credibility with your online audience.
Promote customer loyalty and protection.
Promote customer attraction and retention.

3. Basic principles of online branding:

Brand identity:

Establish a consistent visual identity through logo, color scheme, and typography.

Brand voice:
Set the tone and style of communication, ensuring consistency across all digital channels.

Brand value:
Clearly express and protect the values and principles that the brand represents.

4. Developing a Brand Strategy:

Conducting market research will help you understand your target audience, competitors, and organizational trends.
Define your brand's unique value proposition (USP).
Set clear brand objectives and goals.

5. Online presence and website:

Your website is the focal point of your online brand.
Ensure a website that is user-friendly, responsive, and visually appealing.
Search engine optimization (SEO) to improve visibility.

6. Content marketing and storytelling:

Create valuable, engaging content that aligns with your brand message. Storytelling humanizes your brand, making it accessible and memorable.

Consistently publish blog posts, videos, infographics, and more to demonstrate your expertise.

7. Building a brand on social networks:

 Maintain a consistent presence on appropriate social media platforms.
Maintain consistent branding elements like profile images, cover photos, and messaging. Engage with your audience by responding to comments and messages.

8. Online reputation management:

Monitor online mentions, reviews, and comments.
Respond to negative comments professionally and transparently.
Encourage satisfied customers to leave positive reviews.

9. Influencer Marketing:

 Partner with influencers who share your brand values and target audience.
Influencers can amplify your message and reach a wider audience.

10. Email Marketing:

 - Create personalized email campaigns that reflect your brand voice.
- Use email marketing to nurture leads, promote products, and nurture customer relationships.

11. Paid advertising and brand awareness:

 - Invest in paid advertising campaigns to increase brand awareness.
- Use display advertising, search advertising, and social media advertising.
- Consistency of message and advertising design is essential.

 12. Brand and performance analysis:

 - Use analytics tools to track brand performance metrics like brand awareness, sentiment, and engagement.
- Adjust strategy based on data insights.

 13. Brand principles and standards:

- Develop comprehensive brand guidelines, detailing logo usage, color codes, typography, and brand voice.
- Ensure that all team members and partners adhere to these principles.

14. Adaptation and Evolution:

- Brands must be adaptable to changing consumer preferences and market dynamics.
- Periodically revisit and update your brand strategy to stay relevant.

15. Brand Loyalty and Advocacy:

- Building a strong online brand should ultimately lead to brand loyalty. - Encourage customers to become brand advocates by providing them with special experiences and offers.

16. Building a personal brand:

Individuals, such as entrepreneurs, influencers, and professionals, can also benefit from online branding. Personal branding involves showcasing your expertise, values, and personality to create a unique online presence.

17. User Experience (UX):

A positive user experience on your website and digital platforms is an integral part of brand perception.

Supports intuitive navigation, responsive design, and fast loading times.

18. Crisis management:

Prepare for potential crises that could damage your brand's reputation. Develop a crisis management plan to effectively respond to negative incidents or public relations challenges.

19. Competitive analysis:

Continuously monitor your competitors' online branding strategies.
Gain a competitive advantage by spotting opportunities to differentiate your brand.

20. Localization and global branding:

Tailor your online branding efforts to different markets and regions.
Consider cultural nuances, language, and local preferences.

21. Social responsibility and sustainability:

Adopt social responsibility and sustainability practices that
align with your brand values.
Communicate these initiatives transparently to build a socially
responsible brand.

22. Brand consistency:

Keep branding elements consistent across all channels, from
your website to social media to email marketing.
Consistency creates recognition and trust.

23. Protect employee brands:

Encourage and empower employees to become brand
advocates. They can amplify your brand message and
humanize your business.

24. Customer-centered method:

Put customers at the center of your online branding efforts.
Collect feedback, listen to customer concerns, and adapt your
brand strategy to meet their needs.

25. Brand development and rebranding:

Brand evolution involves incremental changes in your brand
identity and messaging.
Brand renewal is a more significant transformation, often
driven by changes in business goals or public perception.

26. Metrics and ROI:

Measure the return on investment (ROI) of your online branding efforts. Track metrics like brand awareness, customer acquisition costs, customer lifetime value, and social media engagement.

27. Brand storytelling platform:

Explore a variety of storytelling platforms, such as blogs, social media, podcasts, and video content.
Tailor your brand's storytelling based on platform and audience.

28. Testimonials and case studies:

Leverage customer testimonials and case studies to present real-world success stories.
They can be a strong endorsement of your brand's values.

29. Innovation and adaptation:

Always innovate and adapt to emerging technologies and trends in online branding.
Test new strategies to stay ahead of the competition.

30. Legal protection and intellectual property:

Protect your brand's intellectual property, including trademarks and copyrights.

Understand intellectual property laws to prevent infringement
and protect your brand reputation.

In short, a strong online brand is an asset that can have a
significant impact on a business's success in the digital age.
This requires a clearly defined strategy, consistency across all
online touchpoints, and a deep understanding of the target
audience. By investing in online branding, businesses can
make a lasting impression, nurture customer trust, and achieve
long-term growth and recognition in the competitive digital
landscape.
Building a strong online brand is an ongoing process that
requires dedication, creativity, and a deep understanding of
your audience and market. It's not just about creating a catchy
logo or slogan, it's about cultivating a meaningful and
engaging relationship with your target audience. By
continually refining your online brand strategy and
monitoring market developments, you can build a resilient
and influential brand presence in the digital realm.

Chapter Ten
Emerging digital marketing trends

is a dynamic and growing chapter that explores the latest developments and innovations in the digital marketing landscape. As technology and consumer behavior continue to evolve, it is important for businesses that want to stay competitive in the digital age to stay ahead of emerging trends. This comprehensive summary covers the top emerging trends in digital marketing:

1. Artificial Intelligence (AI) and Machine Learning:

AI and machine learning are revolutionizing digital marketing.
AI-powered chatbots provide personalized customer service.
Machine learning algorithms improve ad targeting and content recommendations.

2. Optimize voice search:

The rise of voice-activated devices like smart speakers is changing search behavior.
Marketers should optimize content for voice search, focusing on conversational keywords.

3. The dominance of video marketing:

Video content, especially short-form videos on platforms like TikTok and Instagram Reels, is becoming increasingly important.
Live streaming and interactive video experiences improve engagement.

4. Augmented Reality (AR) and Virtual Reality (VR):

AR and VR technology delivers rich brand experiences. Brands can use AR for virtual try-ons and product visualization. Virtual reality can transport users to exhibition halls or virtual experiences.

5. Conversational Marketing and Chatbots:

Chatbots are used for real-time customer interaction and support.
Conversational marketing focuses on two-way, personalized interactions with customers.

6. Customize content:

Individual users gain experiences through personalized content.
AI-powered content recommendation engines analyze user behavior to recommend relevant content.

7. Social commerce:

E-commerce features are heavily integrated with social media platforms.

Users can shop directly within social apps, simplifying the customer journey.

8. User Generated Content (UGC):

UGC, such as customer-generated reviews, photos, and videos, builds trust and authenticity.
Brands are leveraging UGC in their marketing campaigns and on their websites.

9. Evolution of influencer marketing:

Influencer marketing is evolving from celebrities to micro and nano influencers with niche followings. Authenticity and alignment with brand values are key considerations.

10. Security and data protection:

 - Privacy regulations like GDPR and CCPA are reshaping data collection and use.
- Marketers should prioritize user privacy and transparency in data handling.

11. Programmatic advertising:

- Programmatic advertising uses AI to automate ad buying and placement.
- It enables real-time bidding and precise targeting across multiple channels.

12. Sustainable and ethical marketing:

- Sustainability and ethical practices are becoming key brand differentiators.
- Green marketing and social responsibility initiatives are gaining ground.

13. Mobile-first strategy and mobile optimization:

- Internet usage is heavily dominated by mobile devices.
- Websites, emails, and ads should be optimized for mobile responsiveness.

14. Predictive Analytics and Big Data:

- Predictive analytics leverages Big Data to predict customer trends and behavior. - Businesses use data-driven insights to make strategic decisions.

15. Niche markets and micro markets:

- Targeting niche audiences with specialized products or content is a growing trend.
- Micro markets require appropriate strategies and messages.

16. 5G technology:

- The deployment of 5G networks enables faster mobile Internet speeds and improved user experience.
- Augmented reality and live streaming benefit from 5G connectivity.

17. Blockchain in marketing:

- Blockchain technology can improve the transparency and security of digital advertising.
- It can fight ad fraud and ensure fair compensation for content creators.

18. Game and interactive content:

- Gamification techniques attract users through interactive experiences. - Interactive quizzes, polls, and storytelling create engaging content.

19. Emotional and experiential marketing:

- Brands focus on emotional connections and memorable experiences.
- Emotional storytelling evokes emotions and resonates with listeners.

20. Continuous learning and adaptation:

- Digital marketers must stay agile, continuously learning and adapting to emerging trends.
- Testing and experimentation are essential to stay relevant in a rapidly changing landscape.

In short, the digital marketing landscape is constantly evolving. Staying informed about emerging trends and adopting innovative strategies is essential for businesses that want to grow and connect with their audiences in the digital age. Marketers who effectively take advantage of these emerging trends will be better positioned to achieve their goals and stay ahead of the competition.

Conclusion

We have embarked on an exciting journey through the ever-changing digital marketing landscape. This book serves as a compass, guiding you through the complex web of strategies, tactics, and emerging trends that define success in the digital age. As we reach the pinnacle of this knowledge-rich journey, let us reflect on the transformative insights and wisdom that have accompanied us.

In the digital realm, where change is the only constant, the search for mastery is a constant endeavor. The pages of this book demystify many aspects of digital marketing, giving you the tools and knowledge you need to confidently navigate this dynamic landscape. We begin our exploration by establishing the basics of digital marketing: understanding the digital ecosystem. We explored the intricacies of search engines, social media platforms, email marketing, and content strategy. We've seen how data, analytics, and storytelling converge to create compelling brand stories.

The concept of SEO has been revealed, revealing its central role in the quest for online visibility. We explored the intricacies of on-page and off-page optimization, delving deeper into the technical aspects behind search engine rankings. The chapter "Data-Driven Decision Making and Analytics" highlights the power of insights, allowing you to make informed choices and steer your digital ship to success.

But we don't stop there. In the chapter "Building a Strong Online Brand," we explored the art of creating a brand

identity that resonates with audiences across the digital
spectrum. We analyzed what makes for a strong online
presence and looked at strategies for cultivating brand loyalty
and advocacy.

The journey continues with a deep dive into the world of
"pay-per-click (PPC) advertising". We've harnessed the power
of paid advertising to deliver immediate results and maximize
ROI. We explored bidding strategies, keyword research, and
the dynamic landscape of online advertising platforms.

As we ventured deeper into the digital landscape, we
discovered "Emerging Digital Marketing Trends". Here we
are already witnessing the transformative impact of AI, voice
search, video marketing, augmented reality, and a host of
other innovations. These trends have redefined the rules of
engagement, providing new avenues for brand building and
audience engagement.

Now that we are nearing the end of this chapter in our
journey, it is essential to realize that digital marketing is not a
static field. It is a field of constant evolution, where
adaptability and innovation are the keys to success. The
knowledge you gain from these pages is not an endpoint but a
stepping stone to continued growth and success.

In the digital realm, success isn't just measured by metrics
and conversions; it is also measured by your ability to forge
authentic connections, create value, and navigate
ever-changing trends in consumer behavior. It's about being

agile, responsive, and attuned to the pulse of the digital landscape.

As you close the final pages of "Digital Marketing Mastery," I encourage you to embrace the spirit of continuous learning and adaptation. Stay curious, experiment boldly, and embrace emerging trends with enthusiasm. Remember that mastery is not a destination; it is a journey of perpetual exploration and refinement.

In the vast and ever-expanding universe of digital marketing, the possibilities are limitless. Your success depends not only on the knowledge you've acquired but also on your willingness to innovate, your commitment to ethical practices, and your dedication to building meaningful connections with your audience.

So, as you embark on your digital marketing odyssey, armed with the insights, strategies, and wisdom from this book, know that you possess the tools to craft your narrative of online success. The digital realm is your canvas, and your mastery is the brushstroke that paints the portrait of your brand's journey.

May your journey be filled with innovation, growth, and the exhilarating pursuit of digital marketing mastery. Here's to your online success and the boundless horizons that await you in the ever-evolving world of digital marketing.

As we linger on the concluding notes of "Digital Marketing Mastery:
Crafting Effective Strategies for Online Success," let's delve even deeper into the profound impact this journey has had on your digital acumen and the transformative potential it holds for your future endeavors.

1. Confidently navigate complexity:

In an increasingly complex digital landscape, this book gives you the confidence to navigate the complexities of digital marketing.
Now you have the knowledge and strategies to chart your way through the maze of algorithms, technology, and consumer behavior.

2. The power of wise decisions:

Armed with data-driven insights and analytics, you can now make informed decisions. The ability to decipher metrics and user behavior and adjust your strategy accordingly is a huge asset in the digital sector.

3. Long-term value of the brand:

In an age of ephemeral trends, one constant remains: the lasting value of brand image.
You understand that building a strong online brand is not a one-time endeavor but a long-term commitment that can build awareness and loyalty.

4. Embrace the pace of change:

"Emerging Trends in Digital Marketing" reveals the future possibilities and innovations that are reshaping the digital marketing landscape.
You realize that staying ahead in your field requires you to be willing to embrace change and experiment with new approaches.

5. A comprehensive perspective:

The journey through this book has given you a comprehensive view of digital marketing.
You understand that success is not achieved through a single tactic but through the harmonious coordination of multiple strategies and channels.
6. Ethical and responsible marketing:

This book emphasizes the importance of ethical and responsible marketing practices.
You recognize the importance of privacy, transparency, and social responsibility in the digital age.

7. Lifelong learning and adaptation:

The culmination of this journey is not an endpoint but a threshold towards lifelong learning. You realize that the world of digital marketing is constantly evolving and your ability to adapt and grow is your most valuable asset.

8. Impact beyond business scope:

The skills and knowledge you gain go beyond business operations.
Whether you want to advance your career, advance a cause, or influence society, mastering digital marketing will allow you to make an impact.

9. Join a community of innovators:

As we close this book, you are not alone on this journey.
You join a dynamic community of digital marketers and innovators who share a common quest for knowledge and the pursuit of excellence.

In short, "Mastering Digital Marketing" is more than just a book; It's a transformational journey that equips you with the tools, strategies, and mindset to thrive in the digital age. It reminds us that in this dynamic field, where change is the only constant, your journey to mastery is a never-ending adventure and your ability to impact is infinite. As you move forward on your path, remember that the digital marketing landscape is your canvas, and your mastery is the stroke that shapes your brand's story. Whether you are an entrepreneur, marketer, or digital enthusiast, your journey continues with the promise of innovation, growth, and the exhilarating pursuit of excellence in digital marketing.

So, with the knowledge gleaned from these pages, go ahead and create your own story of digital marketing mastery: a story filled with creativity, adaptability response, and unwavering commitment to achieving success. Your digital journey has just begun and the possibilities are limitless.